VOL. I

UNSPOKEN WATER

AQUAMAN

UNSPOKEN WATER

KELLY SUE DeCONNICK writer
ROBSON ROCHA penciller
DANIEL HENRIQUES inker
SUNNY GHO colorist
CLAYTON COWLES letterer

**ROBSON ROCHA, DANIEL HENRIQUES
& SUNNY GHO** collection cover artists

AQUAMAN CREATED BY PAUL NORRIS

VOL. I

ALEX ANTONE Editor – Original Series
ANDREA SHEA Assistant Editor – Original Series
JEB WOODARD Group Editor – Collected Editions
ROBIN WILDMAN Editor – Collected Edition
STEVE COOK Design Director – Books
LOUIS PRANDI Publication Design
KATE DURRÉ Publication Production

BOB HARRAS Senior VP – Editor-in-Chief, DC Comics
PAT McCALLUM Executive Editor, DC Comics

DAN DiDIO Publisher
JIM LEE Publisher & Chief Creative Officer
BOBBIE CHASE VP – New Publishing Initiatives & Talent Development
DON FALLETTI VP – Manufacturing Operations & Workflow Management
LAWRENCE GANEM VP – Talent Services
ALISON GILL Senior VP – Manufacturing & Operations
HANK KANALZ Senior VP – Publishing Strategy & Support Services
DAN MIRON VP – Publishing Operations
NICK J. NAPOLITANO VP – Manufacturing Administration & Design
NANCY SPEARS VP – Sales
MICHELE R. WELLS VP & Executive Editor, Young Reader

PEFC Certified

This product is from
sustainably managed
forests and controlled
sources

PEFC/29-31-337   www.pefc.org

In the beginning, there was the ocean. The ocean was the source, the rule. What we call land, the exception.

But men are vain. We forgot her. We drew lines in dirt to divide and defend. Became obsessed with nations on islands that exist only by her mercy.

We turned our backs on her, and she returned the favor. One day she will tire of our insolence and reclaim us all...

But not today.

UNSPOKEN WATER
PART 1 OF 5

KELLY SUE DeCONNICK WRITER
ROBSON ROCHA PENCILLER
DANIEL HENRIQUES INKER
SUNNY GHO COLORIST
CLAYTON COWLES LETTERER
ROCHA, HENRIQUES & GHO COVER

ANDREA SHEA ASST. EDITOR
ALEX ANTONE EDITOR
BRIAN CUNNINGHAM GROUP EDITOR

"NAMMA.

"NAMMA FELT NO SHAME.

"SHE **RAGED** AGAINST THE SEA...

"SHE LOATHED THE OCEAN THAT WOULD DARE TO **JUDGE** HER.

WE SENT HER AWAY. TO LIVE OR DIE ON THE ROCKY ISLANDS MILES FROM OUR SHORE.

WE DIDN'T DO IT TO BE **CRUEL**...

WE HOPED THAT SHE WOULD LEARN **HUMILITY** THERE.

BUT WE KEPT SOMETHING. SOMETHING THAT BELONGED TO NAMMA...

THE VILLAGE OF UNSPOKEN WATER.

I THOUGHT YOU WEREN'T SPEAKING TO ME?

I DIDN'T INTEND TO, WEE, BUT WHEN THE OCEAN PARTS RIGHT IN FRONT OF YOU, I THINK IT'S FAIR TO HAVE A FEW QUESTIONS.

I WILL ANSWER THREE.

GOOD WITCH OR BAD WITCH? FIRST QUESTION.

YOU DO HAVE CHEEK.

SIT. YOU'LL BREAK YOUR BACK.

I'M NOT A WITCH, ANDY.

A HYPNOTIST, THEN? A MAGICIAN?

NONE OF THESE THINGS.

I AM AN OLD WOMAN.

I AM MORE THAN YOU SEE, LESS THAN YOU NEED.

WHAT PURPOSE, WEE?

THAT WAS THREE QUESTIONS. DID YOU FORGET HOW TO COUNT, TOO?

I'M NOT PLAYING GAMES!

YOUNG MAN, YOU HAVE NO *IDEA* WHAT YOU'RE ONTO HERE. I SUGGEST YOU MIND YOUR TONE.

THREE QUESTIONS. BEGIN AGAIN. ASK ME WHAT YOU *TRULY* WANT TO KNOW.

WHO AM I?

WE ARE ALL THE SUM OF OUR ACTIONS, ANDY.

THAT'S AN EVASION!

IT WAS A *BAD QUESTION.* TRY AGAIN! SEARCH YOURSELF. IN THIS MOMENT RIGHT NOW, WHAT DO YOU WANT TO KNOW?

IF... IF THERE'S SOMETHING TO ALL THIS INSANITY...

IF YOU REALLY HAVE HAD IT WITHIN YOUR POWER TO GIVE ME BACK MY MEMORY THIS WHOLE TIME...

...WHY HAVE YOU LET ME SUFFER?

YOU OKAY?

I LOOK OKAY?

IN MY DEFENSE, IT'S PRETTY HARD TO TELL.

GO ON BACK OUT, THEN.

NO. NO, I'M...I'M NOT OKAY, EITHER.

I TRIED TO TELL YOU.

YOU TOLD ME I WAS A GIFT FROM THE SEA. A MAN WITH NO PAST, BORN ON THE NIGHT YOU FOUND ME.

THAT CAN'T POSSIBLY BE TRUE.

OH, THEN THE SEA JUST PARTS FOR EVERY OLD FELLA NOW, DOES IT?

FROM WHOM? MY FAMILY? THE ONES WHO RAISED ME TO FEAR MY MUM ONLY TO TOSS ME BACK AT HER FIRST CHANCE THEY GET?

I DON'T KNOW WHO I AM. BUT I MEAN TO FIND OUT.

HOW DO YOU SEE IT, THEN, "ANDY"?

DO TELL.

THAT'S NOT QUITE--

YOU HAVE TO MEET HER SOMEDAY. MAYBE THEY WERE WAITING FOR SOMEONE WHO COULD *PROTECT* YOU.

AND THAT'S *YOU*, IS IT? IS THAT WHAT YOU THINK? I JUST NEED A BIG, STRONG MAN WHO'S AFRAID TO GET RAINED ON--

THAT'S NOT FAIR AND YOU KNOW IT!

I *NEED TO DO THIS!*

I NEED TO KNOW WHERE I CAME FROM. I NEED ANSWERS. AND IF THIS INSANITY IS HOW I GET THEM, THEN *FINE.*

FINE FOR *YOU*. I'M SET JUST AS I AM, THANK YOU VERY MUCH.

CHOP

NO YOU'RE NOT. YOU'RE STUCK IN THIS LITTLE TOWN, WITH YOUR WITCHY CRAP AND A BUNCH OF CRAZY PEOPLE--

--TWO OR TWO *THOUSAND* TIMES YOUR AGE!

YOU DANCE AT THE WATER AND LIGHT CANDLES AND MEANWHILE THE SEA YOU CLAIM TO LOVE IS *DYING*--

WE ALL KNOW IT, BUT WE PRETEND LIKE IT'S NOT HAPPENING BECAUSE WE FEEL POWERLESS TO STOP IT!

WELL, HERE'S YOUR SHOT, CAILLE! YOU WANT TO MAKE A DIFFERENCE, QUIT WITH THE SPELLS AND *DO SOMETHING.*

IF THE SEA CAN PART AND MERMAIDS CAN APPEAR IN CUPS, THEN MAYBE NAMMA *IS* BEHIND ALL THIS--

BLESSED OCEAN, THOSE YOU BROUGHT TO BOW GATHER HERE BEFORE YOU.

VANITY BESET US. WE FORGOT YOU. IN YOUR WISDOM, YOU TOOK US FROM OUR PEOPLES, FROM OUR HOMELANDS...

...TO UNITE AND BE HUMBLED IN YOUR SERVICE.

I AM CHALCHIUHTLICUE...

ACUECUCYOTICIHUATI.

MATLALCUEITL.

LIKE OUR BELOVED OCEAN, I HAVE HAD MANY NAMES AND MANY FACES.

I AM GODDESS OF SEA.

AND STORM.

A man without a past is a sailor blind to the stars.

That night, Caille and I both went to the Old Ones to learn our histories.

PLACE YOUR OFFERING ON THE FIRE, ANDY.

For me, that meant letting some things go.

Ideas I had about how things worked...

Every clan has a story of how the world began.

The stories of others we call "*myths*." But I will tell you something I *know*:

The myths are Truths.

All of them.

Most begin with water.

From water, the World.

From the sea, the Gods.

For the Gods...

UNSPOKEN WATER

PART 3 OF 5

KELLY SUE DeCONNICK WRITER
ROBSON ROCHA PENCILLER
DANIEL HENRIQUES INKER
SUNNY GHO COLORIST
CLAYTON COWLES LETTERER
ROCHA, HENRIQUES &
BRAD ANDERSON COVER

ANDREA   ALEX   BRIAN
SHEA   ANTONE   CUNNINGHAM
ASST. EDITOR   EDITOR   GROUP EDITOR

THE VILLAGE OF UNSPOKEN WATER.

CAILLE...?

LET'S GO, ANDY. BEFORE I CHANGE MY MIND.

You have memories from before you were born...

...that makes the *waves.*

Do you remember now?

HOW YOU FEELIN'?

EVER SINCE YOU FOUND ME, I'VE BELIEVED I ALMOST DIED IN THE WATER.

THAT THE OCEAN TOOK MY HISTORY FROM ME.

AND NOW... I STILL CAN'T REMEMBER ANYTHING FROM BEFORE THE ISLAND--

IF THERE WAS ANYTHING.

OH, THERE WAS. WEE SHOWED ME A RED-HEADED WOMAN IN THE UNSPOKEN WATER...

I CAN'T REMEMBER HER. BUT I RECOGNIZED HER. DOES THAT MAKE SENSE?

AYE.

I'M NOT AFRAID ANYMORE. THE OCEAN IS A PART OF ME. AND THE ANSWERS I NEED...

...THEY'RE A PART OF IT, TOO.

HOW ABOUT YOU? YOU NERVOUS?

NERVOUS TO MEET M'DEAR, SWEET MUM? ONE WHO GOT HERSELF PUNTED OFF THE OLD GOD ISLAND AND THEN, WHEN SHE WANTED TO SEE ME--

--OPTED T'*POISON THE OCEAN* INSTEAD OF, I DUNNO, MAYBE SENDING A CARD? BLOWIN' A HORN OR SOME SUCH?

OHHH, I BET WHEN WE REACH HER ROCK AND ASK HER REAL NICE TO QUIT *KILLIN' THINGS* SHE'LL MAKE US TEA AND WE'LL HAVE A PROPER REUNION.

ME, NERVOUS? SCARED TO DEATH, EVEN?

NAHHH. I'M SURE SHE'S A PEACH.

Before long, the new Gods created newer Gods...

And the World grew. There were trees and stones and weather of every sort.

The World became a bustling place.

The Ocean gave way to Land.

Father Sea was troubled by the rapidity of invention.

This God begat that, begat another.

And soon there were corals and weeds and even new Ocean Gods swimming in his waters.

They itched the old man and he turned irritable at the sensation...and the absence of deference.

His children had *forgotten* him.

The Mother was
heartbroken at th
loss of her husban

She cried the very first tears that day. But grief soon gave way to rage. And her anger tore her apart.

Her body became seven monsters.

And her new children took vengeance on her old.

HA-AHH!

Just when their defeat was all but assured...

Guilt-ridden at what they'd done, the Gods gathered to make amends.

They created you humans, whose blood contains the Ocean, as an everlasting tribute to the Mother and the Father.

You were made in their image.

...But this is not where the story ends.

The one of the Seven called The Cailleach she found on a secret isle peopled with lesser Ocean Gods...

...Gods whose very existence was a painful reminder of her loss.

The Cailleach remnant was too weak to return to her body, so she hid it inside a foundling child, where it could grow strong.

Mother Salt disguised herself as a being called Namma and pretended the child was her own.

She played the lesser gods for fools and left the babe with them to raise.

But when the child grew strong enough...

HOW SO? BY GROWING OLD?

WE SENT *CHILDREN* TO FACE OUR FOE. WE ASKED *THEM* TO DEFEND *OUR* OCEAN.

THEY'RE NOT *CHILDREN*, TANG. ANDY'S NOT EVEN ENTIRELY HUMAN. AND THEY *CHOSE--*

NO. I AM *ASHAMED*, WEE. AND SO ARE YOU.

KNOCK KNOCK KNOCK

SISTER ATABEY...

MY HEART TELLS ME THEY ARE IN DANGER, LOC.

SUPPOSE THEY ARE IN DANGER. DO WE VALUE TWO LIVES OVER THAT OF THE OCEAN?

I WOULD GIVE *MY* LIFE TO SATISFY NAMMA'S FURY. BUT THERE IS NO GUARANTEE IT WOULD STOP HER.

KNOCK
KNOCK
KNOCK

MAC.

REPU. KU.

IT IS NOT OUR SHAME THAT THEY CHOSE TO GO.

IT IS OURS THAT WE CHOSE TO *LET THEM.*

WE WERE *GODS* ONCE. REMEMBER?

I do, of course. It does not befit Gods to shrink when we are tested.

...AND TO INTRODUCE YOU TO YOUR *DAUGHTER.*

WHAT HAVE YOU DONE TO HER?

MY *DAUGHTER?!* THE MORTAL? THE *HUMAN?* SHE IS NOTHING TO ME!

THE GIRL IS A *PLACE.* A PLACE TO HIDE MY CAILLEACH UNTIL IT COULD GROW STRONG ENOUGH TO RETURN TO ME.

NOW THAT YOU HAVE SO KINDLY *DELIVERED* THEM *BOTH,* I WILL RECLAIM WHAT IS MINE AND BE WHOLE AGAIN!

WHAT WILL THAT DO TO CAILLE?

SHE'LL DIE, PROBABLY. HAVING LIVED WITH THE HAG FOR SO LONG, SHE WON'T HAVE THE STRENGTH TO EVEN BREATHE WITHOUT IT.

SOON I WILL SALT THE EARTH AND YOU WILL *ALL DIE SLOWLY* FOR HOW YOUR GODS FAILED ME.

THAT I KILL THE GIRL NOW IS ALL THE MERCY YOU SHALL SEE!

COME TO ME, MY CAILLEACH!

HOW DARE YOU?

GRFF!

ARRRRGHHHH!!!

INSOLENT CHILD!! YOU WILL PAY--

I AM NOT YOUR *CHILD* AND YOU HAVEN'T EARNED MY *RESPECT!*

RIIIP

WHAT'S HAPPENING TO ME?

CAILLE, CAN YOU KEEP IT? TRY TO HOLD IT IN YOU!

NO!

NO! COME TO ME!!

C-CAN'T... Y-YOU...

...CAN'T... C-CAN'T...

YOU CAN'T CLAIM ME!!!

HA HA HA!

WELL PLAYED, BOY, BUT YOU'RE TOO LATE. I HAVE ENOUGH.

YEAH... WELL...

CAN YOU *FEEL* IT? CAN YOU FEEL THE *BITTER WATER* BRINGING *DEATH* TO THE SEA? SALT THE WATER, SALT THE EARTH.

WHEN YOUR WORLD SHRIVELS AND DIES, MY BELOVED WILL FINALLY KNOW *VENGEANCE*!

UNSPOKEN WATER

PART 5 OF 5

KELLY SUE
DECONNICK
WRITER

ROBSON
ROCHA
PENCILLER

DANIEL
HENRIQUES
INKER

SUNNY GHO
COLORIST

CLAYTON COWLES
LETTERER

ROCHA, HENRIQUES
& ALEX SINCLAIR
COVER

ANDREA
SHEA
ASST. EDITOR

ALEX ANTONE
EDITOR

BRIAN
CUNNINGHAM
GROUP EDITOR

You don't know who you are...can't even recall your own true name.

But the Call comes from a place beyond remembrance.

It reaches out to sea-born creatures with *untamed blood*...

...and it echoes inside us.

SKRRRK

KREEEEEEE

I TIRE OF THESE GAMES!

BEGONE, NUISANCE!

AHHHHHH!

I GOT YE!

ANDY!

AHHHHH--

HOLD STILL, KU IS A HEALER.

I-IS THERE S-SOMETHING WE CAN GIVE HER TO MAKE HER GO AWAY?

WHAT DOES SHE WANT?

REVENGE. THE GODS SHE BORE BETRAYED HER AND THE FATHER. IT'S LITTLE WONDER SHE'D SEE US ALL DEAD.

WE
MUUUUST

GIVE
NAAAAAMMA

WHAAAAT
SHE ISSSS
DUUUUE.

TANG, BUDDY,
WE JUST RULED
THAT OUT!

WE'RE NOT
ENDING THE WORLD
TODAY.

NOT THE
WORLD, THE
GODS.

IF HER
HUNGER IS
SATED, PERHAPS
SHE'LL SPARE
YOUR WORLD.

*MOTHER
SALT!* ACCEPT MY
SACRIFICE. WILLINGLY
GIVEN, IN YOUR
HONOR.

WHAT?
WEE, NO!
WHAT ARE YOU
DOING?

CHOOSING
MY FATE.

UNTIL THE NEXT WORLD...

...MY LOVE.

NOOOOOOOO!!!

CAILLE.

WHAT IS HAPPENING? ANDY, CAN YOU HEAR ME?!

ANDY!

CAILLE!

KU, ATTEND HER PAIN.

N-NAMMA'S NOT MY MOTHER, AGWE! THAT'S GOOD AT LEAST, RIGHT?

AND WHAT IF SHE WERE, GIRL? WE ARE ONLY OUR OWN SELVES.

NOT ME. TELL HIM, REPU. THERE'S A MONSTER INSIDE ME. "THE CAILLEACH."

NO, CAILLE.

THERE IS SOMETHING *POWERFUL* INSIDE YOU.

WHETHER IT IS MONSTROUS...

...IS UP TO YOU.

...but not *contained.*

FATHER...

HOW? HOW ARE YOU ALL HERE?

BY THE GRACE OF THE OCEAN. AND WITH GRATITUDE TO YOU.

IT WAS CAILLE'S IDEA.

AND YOUR POWER.

THERE. A GIFT. YOU ARE MARKED AS ONE OF US NOW.

THANK YOU, BUT--A GOD? NO. I STILL DON'T KNOW WHO OR WHAT I AM.

HE MEANS, YOU BELONG TO THE OCEAN.

THE HONOR IS NOT TO *RULE*. IT IS TO *SERVE*.

OUR DEAL STILL STANDS, ANDY.

WHEN WE RETURN TO THE VILLAGE, YOU MAY DRINK OF THE *UNSPOKEN WATER*.

WE WILL FIND OUT *WHO* YOU ARE SOON ENOUGH.

BUT *WHAT* YOU ARE? I CAN TELL YOU THAT.

YOU ARE A HERO...AND A *FRIEND*.

ANDY, YOU HAVE ONE MORE GIFT TO RECEIVE...

VARIANT COVER GALLERY

AQUAMAN #43 variant cover by **NICOLA SCOTT** and **ANNETTE KWOK**

SKETCHBOOK BY **ROBSON ROCHA**

BROWN
LEATHER
BELT

GOD OF
OCEANS

GODDESS OF
EARTH

Robson

Robson

NAMMA

SALT FORM

GOD OF
OCEANS

GODDESS OF
EARTH

Robson

Robson

VARUNA
HUMAN

GOD

TANG

GOD FORM

KU   GOD FORM

ROBSON

AMAN HUMAN GOD

ROBSON

ATABEY GOD

HUMAN

ROBSON

AGWE

HUMAN
↓

GOD
↓

MAC
HUMAN
↓

GOD
↓

PENCILLER Robson Rocha   INKER _____   PAGE# 13
TITLE Aquaman   ISSUE # 43   MONTH _____   INTERIORS

PENCILLER ROBSON ROCHA   INKER
TITLE AQUAMAN   ISSUE # 45   PAGE# 07   MONTH
INTERIORS

PENCILLER Robson Rocha   INKER   PAGE # 17   INTERIORS
TITLE AQUAMAN   ISSUE # 46   MONTH